21st CENTURY LIVES
TV CELEBRITIES

Liz Gogerly

WAYLAND

First published in 2007 by Wayland

Reprinted in 2008 and 2009

© Copyright 2007 Wayland

Wayland
338 Euston Road
London NW1 3BH

Wayland Australia
Level 17/207 Kent Street
Sydney NSW 2000

Editor: Claire Shanahan
Designer: Fiona Grant
Design: Peter Bailey for Proof Books
Cover Design: Hodder Children's Books

British Library Cataloguing in Publication Data
 Gogerly, Liz
   TV Celebrities. - (21st Century Lives)
   1. Television personalities - Juvenile literature
   I. Title
   791.4'5'0922

ISBN 978 0 7502 5240 9

Printed in China

Wayland is a division of Hachette Children's Books, an Hachette UK company.

www.hachette.co.uk

Contents

Ant and Dec
TV's top mates

Ant and Dec as pop duo PJ and Duncan. The boys claim that they treated being pop stars like the next acting job.

> **"I think we're nice people and nice professionally but you know we're not... what's the word: It's not as if we're just grinning idiots, know-what-I-mean? When decisions have got to be made, they'll be made."**

Ant McPartlin
The Guardian, September 2005

Names: Anthony David McPartlin
Declan Joseph Oliver Donnelly

Dates and places of birth:
Ant: 18 November 1975, Newcastle upon Tyne, England
Dec: 25 September 1975, Newcastle upon Tyne, England

Big break: Ant made his television debut on children's entertainment programme *Why Don't You?* Dec made his television entrance on the children's drama series *Byker Grove* in 1989. Ant joined him there a year later.

Top television moments:
There was high drama in *Byker Grove* when PJ, played by Ant, was blinded in both eyes in a paintballing accident. His best mate Duncan, played by Dec, asked him, "PJ, what's it like to be blind?". This line was much repeated as a joke in the 1990s. Other top moments include *The Ant & Dec Show, Ant & Dec's Saturday Night Takeaway* and *I'm a Celebrity, Get Me Out of Here!.*

Style: Ant and Dec love to banter and take the 'mick' out of each other and anyone else. This humour is possibly the secret of their success.

Awards: In 2002, the duo received a joint Special Recognition Award at the National Television Awards (NTAs). They've also scooped the Best Entertainment Presenter awards eight years on the trot at the NTAs.

Star quality: Their genuine 'mateyness' towards each other. This seems to bring them closer to the viewer too!

Something you might not know about them:
On television and in photographs, Ant is mostly on the left and Dec is on the right. They admit it feels strange if they don't do it this way round.

The likeable duo Ant and Dec have been on our television screens since the 1980s. In that time they've covered drama, pop music and presenting, and they've even given film a go.

Ant and Dec lived close to each other as children, but they never knew one another. Ant was a bright boy who helped to look after his younger sisters when his father walked out. He's a great cook to this day! He took up acting at school. Dec is the youngest of seven children. He auditioned for the part in *Byker Grove* when he saw it advertised in a newspaper.

The boys met on the set of *Byker Grove*, but they didn't like each other straight away. They were best friends in the script and gradually they became mates off-screen too. The duo became the stars of the show. When at 18 they were written out of the story, it was a shock that spurred them on to the next chapter of their careers. Ant and Dec emerged as boy band PJ and Duncan. They went on to have 16 hit singles and three platinum-selling albums.

After PJ and Duncan came the successful *Ant and Dec Show* on the BBC. Meanwhile, Ant and Dec set up Ant and Dec Productions and came up with the idea for *SMTV Live* and *CD:UK*. These shows turned them into stars of ITV's children's programmes.

By 2001, Ant and Dec had their eyes on the next challenge. Their role model was Noel Edmonds. He'd made the leap successfully from children's television to family entertainment and they wanted to follow his example. Their hit shows *I'm a Celebrity, Pop Idol, Poker Face* and *Ant & Dec's Saturday Night Takeaway* are proof of their lasting popularity, but also of their ability to move with the times.

Over the years Ant and Dec returned to acting. In 2002, they starred in a remake of the old comedy *The Likely Lads*. The following year they appeared in the movie *Love Actually*. Then, in 2006, they got good reviews for their parts in the film *Alien Autopsy*. Ant and Dec may only be in their 30s, but they seem to have been on our screens forever. And it looks like they're here to stay for years to come.

Ant and Dec celebrate receiving the award for Most Popular Entertainment Presenter at the National Television Awards ceremony in 2005.

"It's so sweet watching them together, isn't it? They're like an old married couple."

Prince Harry
The Observer, May 2006

Billie Piper
Award-winning actress

Billie attends a book signing for her autobigraphy Growing Pains *– published when she was 23!*

❝ When I was younger I was so ambitious. I'm still ambitious now, but I don't have the hunger I did, say, when I was 10 years old. I was certainly more fearless then, and more selfish, and just wanted to do exceptionally well. ❞

Billie Piper
The Guardian, December 2006

Name: Registered at birth as Lianne Piper, but within weeks her parents changed her name to Billie

Date and place of birth: 22 September 1982, Swindon, England

Big break: Billie starred in a television advertisement for the pop magazine *Smash Hits* when she was 15. She caught the eye of agents at the record company Virgin who were looking for a new artist to appeal to young girls.

Top television moments: Billie's highlight to date has been playing Rose Tyler in *Doctor Who*. She became as popular as the doctor himself.

Style: Down-to-earth with her head firmly on her shoulders. Despite her youth, she always appears mature in interviews.

Awards: Billie has scooped numerous best actress awards for her portrayal of Rose in *Doctor Who*. In 2005 and 2006, she won the National Television Award and the BBC Drama Award for best actress.

Star quality: Billie is a true professional with a love of acting. She likes to roll up her sleeves and just get on with it.

Something you might not know about her: The morning after her first date with the DJ Chris Evans, she woke up to find a silver Ferrari parked outside her house. The car was his gift to her and it was filled with red roses. Soon afterwards, they ran away to get married in Las Vegas in the USA.

Billie holds the award for most popular actress at the British Academy TV Awards in 2006. She won the award for her part in Doctor Who.

touch with her parents. She disappeared from the public eye and began to rebuild her life. Billie came through the difficult times and made a brief comeback to the music business.

The next thing we heard about Billie was her whirlwind romance and marriage to multi-millionaire broadcaster and DJ Chris Evans. For Billie, this was a turning point in her life. She found the inner strength to pursue her original dream of becoming an actress and enrolled at acting school in Los Angeles, in the USA.

In 2003, Billie made her acting debut in the BBC dramatisation of *The Canterbury Tales*. Her performance earned her many positive reviews. The year 2005 was a bumper year in which Billie impressed audiences in the long-awaited return of *Doctor Who*. She also played Hero in a modern version of Shakespeare's *Much Ado About Nothing*. On a sad note Billie and Chris Evans announced their divorce, but to this day remain close friends.

In 2006, Billie made the shocking decision to leave *Doctor Who* after just two series. Next came major parts in Philip Pullman's *The Ruby in the Smoke* and Jane Austen's *Mansfield Park*. The following year, she received excellent reviews for her stage debut in *Treats*. Billie has proved she can make the leap from pop star to actress – many critics think the next jump will be to film star.

Billie Piper is often likened to 'the girl next door' but she has a face you can't forget. She burst onto the scene over a decade ago as a pop singer. Now she's one of the most talented actresses around.

Billie is the daughter of Paul and Mandy Piper, a builder and housewife from Swindon. She is the oldest of four children and was desperate to leave home and get on with adult life. She dreamed of becoming an actress and joined the Sylvia Young Theatre School. A bit part in *Eastenders* followed, but at 15 her acting career was put on hold.

Billie signed with Virgin in 1998 and released her first single, *Because We Want To*. The song went to number one, making her the youngest person to achieve a debut number one in the UK. She went on to have two more number one hit singles and three top-selling albums. However, by 1999, Billie was struggling with stardom. She developed an eating disorder and lost

"In *The Miller's Tale* she was playing a singer, married to an older man. But, for all that, there was clearly proper acting going on. People came to me time and time again, saying she blew them away. Now whenever I'm in casting discussions, her name always comes up."

Peter Bowker, writer for BBC production of *The Canterbury Tales*.
The Telegraph, November 2005

Simon Cowell
King of reality TV

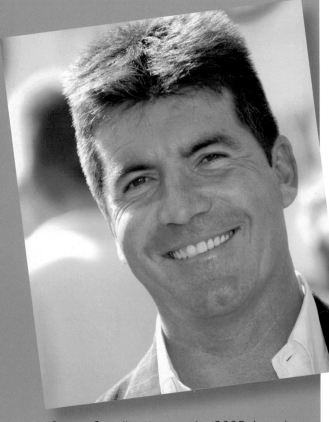

Simon Cowell arrives at the 2005 American Idol *Final. He claims to treat the talent show like a business in which he uses his head rather than his heart to make decisions.*

> **"People come up to me and sing, and I say, 'That was great. Thank you.' And they're like, 'Well, aren't you going to be rude to me?' No. 'Well, can you be rude to me?' No! They expect me to be cruel to them – it's some sort of badge of honour. That's how crazy everything is."**

**Simon Cowell
January 2007**

Name: Simon Philip Cowell

Date and place of birth:
7 October 1959, Brighton, England

Big break: Simon's career kicked off in the music industry. He worked for major record companies and started his own music companies. Before his break in television, he was most famous for signing Westlife, the record-breaking, Irish boy band.

Top television moments:
Simon has appeared in *Pop Idol, American Idol, World Idol* and *The X Factor*. He has become infamous for his straight talking. When he's in the judge's seat, he isn't scared to tell the contestant what he really thinks. Some of his most memorable comments (and therefore best television moments) are, "You have just invented a new version of torture", "You should sue your music teacher" and, "You look like the Incredible Hulk's wife".

Style: He's brutally honest with bursts of wit and warmth. He's also vain – on a recent episode of the Radio 4 programme *Desert Island Discs*, he requested a mirror as his luxury item if he ever found himself stuck on a desert island.

Star quality: His honesty. Simon is a businessman who knows that, to succeed, you sometimes have to be cruel to be kind.

Something you might not know about him:
Simon made a guest appearance in an episode of *The Simpsons*. In the episode *Smart and Smarter,* Homer Simpson has harsh words with Mr Cowell when he makes his daughter Maggie cry during an audition for nursery school.

Simon Cowell is the TV personality most of us love to hate. He claims that his honest outbursts on *Pop Idol* and *The X Factor* are not meant to be nasty. He just wants to find the winner.

In his own career, Simon has had to fight his way to the top. Life started well enough. He was raised in Elstree, Hertfordshire, by his parents Eric and Julie Cowell. His father was a property developer and music industry executive for EMI Music Publishing. From an early age, Simon was used to famous faces popping round to his house. When he left school at 17, he found it difficult to settle down in a job. Eventually his father got him a position at EMI.

Simon worked his way through the ranks at EMI to become a record producer. During the 1980s, Simon set up two of his own music companies but unfortunately these both flopped. In 1989, he was bankrupt and living back at home with his parents. A new career with record company BMG restored his fortunes. As well as Westlife, he signed chart-toppers 5ive and Curiosity Killed the Cat. He was also behind hits for the Teletubbies and the Power Rangers!

By 2001, Simon Cowell had become one of the most powerful men in the music industry. He seemed like an obvious choice to become one of the judges on a new reality talent show called *Pop Idol*. In the first season of the show the public was introduced to his nasty streak. He insulted the contestants, but his criticism was also constructive. At the end of the series his record company S Records signed the winner, Will Young, and the runner-up, Gareth Gates. Simon's special brand of arrogance and brutal honesty won him a place in the USA version of the show, *American Idol*.

Simon has gone on to set up his own production company, Syco. This is behind the popular reality talent show *The X Factor*, in which Simon also stars. The brand has been imported to America where Simon Cowell is as much a household name as he is in Britain. Meanwhile, Simon hasn't lost his flair for coming up with new ideas for popular programmes. In 2007, Syco launched a successful new competition show in the USA called *American Inventor*. Meanwhile, in the UK, there was a new show to find the cast for a production of the musical *Grease* and *Britain's Got Talent* aired on ITV1.

Simon Cowell with The X Factor *presenter Louis Walsh, the 2004 winner, Steve Brookstein, and runner-ups, G4.*

"Unlike the wannabes on *Pop Idol*, Simon Cowell is among that rare breed of TV talent who is virtually guaranteed success just by turning up."

MediaGuardian, July 2004

The Osbournes
Rock 'n' roll family

Back in black: The Osbourne family at the 2004 Grammy Awards.

> ❝ **I'm about caring, I'm about people, and I'm about entertaining people. I'm a family man. A husband. A father. I've been a lot of other things over the years, which we don't really want to talk about. I'm always working on trying to better myself, you know? I think I'll do that for the rest of my life. I'm always thinking of what I can do today to better my life...** ❞
>
> **Ozzy Osbourne**

Names: Ozzy Osbourne (born John Michael Osbourne)
Sharon Rachel Osbourne (maiden name Arden)
Kelly Michelle Lee Osbourne
Jack Joseph Osbourne

Dates and places of birth:
Ozzy: 3 December 1948, Birmingham, England
Sharon: 9 October 1952, London, England
Kelly: 27 October 1984, London, England
Jack: 8 November 1985, London, England

Big break: Ozzy was the first star in the family. He was lead singer with heavy rock band Black Sabbath and then a mega solo success. The whole family stepped into the limelight when they starred in the television reality show *The Osbournes,* which ran on MTV from 2002 to 2005.

Top television moments:
The first episode of *The Osbournes* features the family moving into their swanky mansion in Beverly Hills. The chaos, swearing, fighting and the making-up scenes were a taste of what was to come.

Style: Outrageously wild and loving.

Awards: In 2002, *The Osbournes* won an Emmy in the USA, for the Outstanding Non-fiction Programme. The following year it was nominated for a National Television Award in the UK.

Star quality: A dysfunctional but strangely ordinary bunch. What can be more pleasing than watching the rock icon Ozzy Osbourne, aka The Prince of Darkness, taking the rubbish out or trying to tune a DVD player?

Something you might not know about them:
To date, Sharon's explicit memoir, *Extreme,* is the bestselling hardback autobiography since records began.

The Prince of Darkness with his famous family appears on MTV in 2002.

In 2002, television viewers were glued to their screens when MTV launched its new fly-on-the-wall show *The Osbournes*. This programme promised to be like no other – it followed the antics of the wild man of rock and his equally crazy family.

The Osbournes was aired on MTV and later on Channel 4 in the UK. After the first episode it became an international hit and ran for three series. It was a riveting mix of reality show and sitcom, with the family all appearing to be natural comedians. The swearing, the arguments and the crises were all larger than life in the Osbourne household. But amongst the chaos were moments of sensitive family drama. In the final series, Jack and Kelly fought to overcome drug addictions, Sharon battled cancer and Ozzy recovered from injuries from a bike crash in which he nearly died.

The Osbournes turned the whole family into mega celebrities. Ozzy was already famous but now Sharon, Kelly and Jack were in demand too. When the show finished in 2005, all the Osbournes were pursuing other television or musical projects. In 2003, Sharon hosted her own talk show in the USA called *The Sharon Osbourne Show*, but it was soon axed. The UK Version, launched in 2006, had a similar fate. More successful was Sharon's appearance on the reality talent show *The X Factor*, but she left the show in 2008.
While Sharon attracts big audiences on primetime television, her children's careers are also shaping up.

Jack hosts *Jack Osbourne: Adrenaline Junky* on ITV2. In the show, he is seen trying out a number of extreme sports. He's also presented *Union Jack* for Channel 4. Meanwhile, Kelly has released three albums and had a number one hit single with *Changes*, a song she recorded with her father. She has presented *I'm a Celebrity, Get Me Out of Here! Now!* and *Project Catwalk* on television, DJs on Radio1 and presented the 2008 Brit Awards with the rest of the Osbourne clan. Never one to stand in the background, Ozzy headlines his own free festival, Ozzfest, each year in the UK and USA, and he released a new album in 2007. Ozzy might be slightly deaf, but he's still ready to rock.

"If you take out the profanity, the TV show *The Osbournes* is a show about good family values."

American chat show host Jay Leno

Fearne Cotton

TV's top presenter

Fearne Cotton at the National Television Awards in 2006.

Name: Fearne Cotton

Date and place of birth:
3 September 1981, London, England

Big break: At 16 Fearne was picked to present ITV's children's show *The Disney Club*. She claims she went to loads of auditions before she was spotted.

Top television moments:
On 2 July 2005, Fearne Cotton presented *Live 8* in the UK. One of the performers at the benefit concert was the pop star Robbie Williams. Viewers were squirming in their seats when Robbie said to Fearne, "You're single, I'm single, I live in LA, I've got dogs, come and live with me in LA, let's get it on!". Nobody knew for sure if Robbie meant it. It was a classic television moment. Fearne later said, "I've always cheekily fancied him".

Style: She's loud and sassy but she usually looks fantastic in her cool, exceptionally trendy, second-hand clothes.

Awards: In 2004, Fearne picked up the Caron Keating Young Presenter of the Year award at the Variety Club Show Business Awards.

Star quality: Playful and go-getting, she's one of the lads but girls like her style.

Something you might not know about her:
She has an A' level in art and relaxes by painting. She also takes good care of herself by doing reiki and meditation.

> **" I do believe that you can do anything you want if you work hard enough, but you have to think about how to get there. Just saying, 'I want to be famous' isn't enough. That's got to involve thinking about what school subjects might help; how you could get a behind-the-scenes job, anything. And then you've got to work really hard. "**
>
> **Fearne Cotton**
> *The Guardian, April 2004*

Fearne worked with ITV for four years. During that time she got to present programmes about art and craft, including *Draw Your Own Toons* and *Finger Tips*. A move to the BBC followed where Fearne presented *Eureka TV* before moving on to weekend shows like *Smile* and *The Saturday Show*.

As a music fan and keen dancer, Fearne was thrilled to present the primetime music show *Top of the Pops*. She was the main presenter from 2003 until the show went off air in 2006. Her association with all things pop continued with jobs presenting *Live 8* in London in 2005, reading out the votes for the UK at the 2006 *Eurovision Song Contest* and interviewing guests backstage at the 2007 *Brits*. Fearne also loves fashion and was chosen to present the reality TV show *Make Me A Supermodel*. An eye for fashion means she was an ideal new presenter for the UK coverage of the Oscars in 2007.

Fearne is also passionate about her involvement in fundraising programmes such as *Children In Need* and *Comic Relief*. In 2003, she took part in *Comic Relief Does Fame Academy*. In 2005, she went to Kenya to visit children living on the streets. She met children with AIDS and drug addiction problems.

When Fearne isn't working on television she is a Radio 1 DJ. In her spare time she likes to paint and is currently working on a collection of portraits of pop stars for an exhibition.

Fearne presents the Brits Launch Party with comedian Russell Brand in 2007.

Fearne Cotton's career began in children's television. Later, she became the bubbly, fashionably-clad presenter of *Top of the Pops*. Recently she presented the UK coverage of the Oscars, the biggest Hollywood event of the year. Is there no stopping this fun-loving girl from London?

Fearne Cotton is the daughter of Lyn and Mick Cotton. She was raised in north-west London, where her father ran his own sign-writing company. She was a busy child and filled her time with Brownies, ballet and drama classes. At school she was a rebel and was always the loudest girl in the class.

In 1998, Fearne's gift for talking got her noticed in a national search for new presenters. She was just 16 when she began her television career on ITV's early-morning children's programme, *The Disney Club*.

"I think if you're looking for a way into presenting the best thing to do is go to a drama club at school or at the weekend… They teach you confidence and discipline so you know you have to put the work in to get where you want to go."

Fearne Cotton

David Tennant
The all new Doctor Who

The part of Doctor Who earned David Tennant the award for Best Actor at the National Television Awards in 2006.

> **" I was very small, about three or four I think, and just wanted to be the people on telly telling these wonderful stories... I can't ever remember wanting to do anything else. I've just sort of taken it for granted all my life that that was what I would do. "**

David Tennant

Name: David John McDonald – he took the stage name Tennant after reading an interview in *Smash Hits* with the singer Neil Tennant from the band the Pet Shop Boys

Date and place of birth:
18 April 1971, West Lothian, Scotland

Big break: In 2005, he took his first lead role in the television drama *Casanova* and worked his way into viewer's hearts.

Top television moments:
Playing the tenth Doctor in the television series *Doctor Who* is like a dream come true for David, who has wanted to play the character since he was three years old. His classic moment is his passionate kiss with Madame de Pompadour, the mistress of King Louis XV, in the episode *The Girl in the Fireplace*.

Style: David brings energy and intensity to all his roles. In *Casanova* he is a boyish and seductive lover, but in the drama *Secret Smile* he is a thoroughly nasty psycho.

Awards: In 2005, he won an award for the Best Male Performance from the Critics for Theatre in Scotland for his part in *Look Back in Anger*. In 2006 and 2008, he won the National Television Award for Best Actor for his part in *Doctor Who*.

Star quality: He's a chameleon, who can switch on the charm, exude evil or ham up his act to make it funny.

Something you might not know about him:
In 2006, David took part in *Ready, Steady, Cook* with his father. It seems David is a much better actor than a cook!

David Tennant is probably best known for playing the tenth Doctor Who, but there's more to him than being a travelling Time Lord.

Acting has been in David's blood since he was a child. He was raised in Ralston, Renfrewshire in Scotland. As a boy he tuned into episodes of *Doctor Who*. His obsession with the Doctor turned into a burning desire to become an actor. His father, the Reverend Alexander McDonald, the minister of the local church, did his best to discourage him, as he was concerned about David making a living on the stage. David did well at school but he didn't listen to his father. After leaving school he enrolled at the Royal Scottish Academy of Music and Drama in Glasgow to train as an actor.

After drama school, David joined the 7.84 Theatre Company. The group performed agitprop, a type of political drama that aims to cut through propaganda and agitate or make people think about the state of the world. His first professional part was in *The Resistible Rise of Arturo Uri*, which also starred Ashley Jensen of *The Office* fame. In 1996, he began working with the Royal Shakespeare Company where he excelled in comic parts.

In 2004, David appeared as Mr Gibson, a rather slimy vicar in the drama adaptation of Anthony Trollope's *He Knew He Was Right*. People began to sit up and notice the promising young Scottish actor. This was a good year for David as he was also on screen playing a lovesick detective in the BBC drama *Blackpool*. Meanwhile, he was busy working on the dramas *Casanova* and *The Quatermass Experiment*, and the film *Harry Potter and The Goblet of Fire* as Bartemius Crouch Junior.

Doctor Who made its comeback to television in 2005. The classical actor Christopher Eccleston was chosen as the new Doctor Who. David had been on the list of candidates to play the Doctor, so when Christopher made the shock decision to leave after just one series, David stepped into his shoes. He has brought something new to the character and has been praised for his light and jaunty touch. Meanwhile, David refuses to be pigeonholed as the Doctor and announced his intention to leave the show in 2008. David Tennant most recently appeared as Hamlet for the Royal Shakespeare Company.

Theatre remains important to David. He regularly acted with the Royal Shakespeare Company. Here, he plays Captain Jack Absolute in Sheridan's Rivals.

"David can go from geeky copper to handsome lover in just one moment – and I think he knows when he's doing it. That's the sign of a great actor. He's very good at capturing those moments when you find yourself surprisingly drawn to someone emotionally."

Peter Bowker, writer of *Blackpool*.
The Guardian, January 2005

Catherine Tate
Comic genius

Catherine Tate arrives at the 2006 National Television Awards where her show was nominated for the award for comedy.

"Although I was a shy child, I was also a bit flamboyant. And that used to make people laugh, which was important at a self-conscious age. I realised that if you get yourself labelled as the funny one, people don't look any further. I decide what part of my personality you're seeing. I don't want you to look at me, I really don't. I don't want you to comment on my clothes, my hair or the way I look."

Catherine Tate, *The Independent*, December 2006

Name: Born Catherine Ford, she changed her name when she became an actress

Date and place of birth: 12 May 1968, London, England

Big break: In 2000, Catherine starred in the *New Brits* show at the Edinburgh Festival. It was here that a comedy scout from the BBC spotted her. The following year she appeared in a sitcom called *Wild West*, starring opposite the successful comedian Dawn French.

Top television moments: In three series of *The Catherine Tate Show*, she has made us laugh with some of her amazing characters. Her most well-known character is Lauren Cooper, the cockney teenager with her famous catchphrase "Am I bovvered?". Joannie 'Nan' Taylor, the naughty grandmother who can't stop swearing, is also popular.

Style: Catherine can do straight acting, but she is most famous for her comic characters.

Awards: Catherine won the Best Comedy Newcomer award at the 2004 British Comedy Awards. This was for the first series of *The Catherine Tate Show*. In 2006, she scooped the Best British Comedy Actress award at the British Comedy Awards for the second series of the show.

Star quality: She makes it look so easy! And, with Catherine, you never know what or who is coming next.

Something you might not know about her: Catherine doesn't like the limelight. She is quite a shy and nervous person. When she attended the Variety Club Awards in London in 2005, she avoided the red carpet at the front of the hotel and chose to enter round the back.

Catherine Tate as Lauren the teenager at ASDA's 2005 'Tickled Pink' Annual Charity Concert to raise funds for breast cancer.

Catherine had to wait until 2004 before the first series of *The Catherine Tate Show* was broadcast. Stroppy teenager Lauren and naughty 'Nan' Taylor became instant favourites with her audience. "I created a monster", Catherine says of Lauren, "but you can't moan about things that are successful". *The Catherine Tate Show* has gone on to become one of the most popular shows on BBC2 and Catherine has made appearances as Lauren in the 2005 *Comic Relief* show and *Children in Need* programme. One of Catherine's top moments was playing Lauren before the Queen and Prince Philip at the 2005 Royal Variety Performance. She looked up at the Queen's box and asked, "Is one bovvered? Is one's face bovvered?". In 2007, as part of *Red Nose Day*, Lauren appeared alongside Prime Minister Tony Blair.

As a classically trained actor, Catherine is determined she won't just be remembered as a comedian or Lauren the teenager. She has acted with the Royal Shakespeare Company and in 2005 appeared on stage alongside *Friends* star David Schwimmer in the play *Some Girl(s)*. At Christmas 2006, she made an appearance in *Doctor Who* as a bride. This led to a stint as the Doctor's companion throughout the fourth season. In early 2007, she took a leading part in the TV drama *The Bad Mother's Handbook*. With film appearances and commissions to write television drama, it looks like Catherine Tate is here to stay…

Catherine Tate is famous for making us laugh, but behind the many funny faces is a serious actor bursting to get out!

Catherine was raised in London by her mother and grandmother. While she was a teenager, she decided she wanted to become an actress. When she left school, she auditioned four times before she was accepted at the Central School of Speech and Drama in London.

After college came a string of bit parts in popular television dramas such as *The Bill*, *Men Behaving Badly* and *Casualty*. It was when Catherine turned her talents to stand-up comedy that she was plucked from obscurity. Originally, she became a comedian to pay the bills, but her successful stint at the 2000 Edinburgh Festival earned her a nomination for a Perrier Award. It also got her noticed by the BBC who quickly signed her up for her own series.

"She has described herself as a lazy control freak. But when the time comes to do it [perform], she changes. Her brain moves incredibly fast when she's performing, she's completely focused."

Geoffrey Perkins, the BBC scout who spotted Catherine Tate at the 2000 Edinburgh Festival. *The Guardian*, December 2005

Richard Hammond
Car-crazy presenter

Richard Hammond arrives at the 2004 TV Moments Awards ceremony in London.

" If we weren't doing *Top Gear* we'd still be out there buying cars and arguing about them. When the cameras stop rolling we carry on arguing – it's what we do! Ultimately, we're three ordinary blokes who love cars. "

Richard Hammond
Auto Trader, April 2006

Names: Richard Mark Hammond

Date and place of birth:
19 December 1969, Birmingham, England

Big break: Richard's career in broadcasting began at BBC Radio York. In 1998, he had his television breakthrough presenting *Motorweek* on the satellite channel Men and Motors.

Top television moments:
In September 2006 whilst filming for *Top Gear*, Richard was taking part in a bid to break the British land speed record in a jet-propelled car. The attempt went disastrously wrong when the car crashed at 280 mph. Richard was rushed to hospital in an air ambulance. His life hung in the balance for a week. However, in January 2007, Richard returned to a hero's welcome at *Top Gear*. Footage of the accident was shown for the first time on the show. Richard's courageous return to the programme has to go down as a top television moment.

Style: A daredevil behind the wheel and a sharp wit in front of the camera.

Star quality: Enthusiasm and drive!

Something you might not know about him:
If Richard wasn't a television presenter he would run a classic car garage. The only problem would be that he and his wife Amanda wouldn't be able to sell any of the cars. Both of them love motors too much, and have a huge collection including a Porsche 997 Carrera S, 1971 Midget, 1972 Spitfire, 68 Ford Mustang, Morgan V6 Roadster, Vauxhall Firenza and 1984 Land Rover Defender (to name but a few!).

A week after his near-fatal crash Richard Hammond manages a smile for members of the Yorkshire Air Ambulance.

Richard Hammond claims to be just an ordinary bloke who happens to love cars. But, his miraculous recovery, following the near fatal car crash in 2006, has turned him into more of a hero than he'd care to admit.

In 1989, when he got his BTEC National Diploma in Visual Communications from Harrogate College of Art and Technology, Richard's dream was to work on television presenting programmes about cars. It was nearly a decade later when he finally popped up on television screens and then it was via satellite. In the meantime, Richard had presented radio programmes and even spent time in the press office of a large corporate company. He returned to journalism because he missed the buzz of chasing a story. Luckily, in 1998, he scored the job with the channel Men and Motors. For a few years he appeared on other satellite channels presenting various lifestyle programmes, then in 2002 he achieved the dream – he joined *Top Gear*.

Richard has test-driven some of the fastest cars in the world at *Top Gear*. He's raced 4X4 vehicles against jet-powered kayaks. He's sat in a car which has been bombarded by artificial lightning. Most gruesome of all, was his crash in September 2006. Richard's fight for life made headline news. At first doctors expected him to die. When he survived there was talk of brain damage. Richard has bravely defied the odds. He worked hard to gain his memory back. Part of his therapy was playing the card game Top Trumps and building with

Lego. When he was finally allowed home, the first car he chose to drive was his Morgan V6 Roadster.

A love of cars is in Richard's blood, but he has presented other types of programme. He hosted three series of *Brainiac: Science Abuse* on Sky One. Later, he presented the dog show *Crufts* (he has four dogs of his own). In 2006, he was back with more motoring mayhem in the quiz *Petrol Heads*, which was hosted by Neil Morrissey. The same year he hosted *Richard Hammond's 5 O'Clock Show* on ITV.

"He is a wonderful, unique and distinctive *Top Gear* presenter. He has brought an awful lot to the programme and his indefatigable energy, the fact that he tries absolutely anything once, may have been the reason that he has overstepped the mark a bit."

Ex-*Top Gear* presenter Quentin Wilson.
The Guardian Unlimited, September 2006

Tess Daly and Vernon Kay
TV's golden couple

The glamorous husband and wife team Vernon Kay and Tess Daly at the National Television Awards 2006 in London.

> **❝I will never get used to the glamorous side of this job, I will never take it for granted and I hope it will never change me. I've always been a northern 'hello chuck' kind of girl. And you can't get more down to earth than northerners – we know who we are and where we're from.❞**
>
> **Tess Daly**
> *Daily Mirror*, **November 2006**

Names: Helen Elizabeth Tess Daly
Vernon Charles Kay

Dates and places of birth:
Tess: 27 April 1971, Stockport, England
Vernon: 28 April 1974, Manchester, England

Big break: While Tess was working as a model, she starred in two videos for the pop band Duran Duran. Her television break came in 1999 when she appeared in Channel 4's *The Big Breakfast*. Vernon's big break came when he was spotted by a model scout for the BBC programme *Clothes Show Live*. His first television break was the BBC children's programme *FBI*.

Top television moments:
Working together as the famous husband and wife team on *Just the Two of Us*, a celebrity singing contest.

Style: Upbeat and totally down-to-earth. Their broad northern accents also set them apart from other presenters.

Awards: None as yet but they were both up for the most popular entertainer award at the 2005 National Television Awards, making them the first married couple to be nominated for the same award in the competition.

Star quality: Model good looks and a natural ease with both guests and the audience.

Something you might not know about them:
In February 2007, the couple became patrons of Great Ormond Street, the famous children's hospital in London. They are regular visitors to the patients at the hospital and are also involved in fundraising events.

Vernon Kay has been named the next Bruce Forsythe and Tess Daly is heralded as the golden girl of Saturday night television. They are glamorous and gorgeous, but they are also down-to-earth and genuine.

In September 2003, Vernon and Tess were married near his hometown of Bolton. The perfect pair seem made for one another. They share a love of entertainment and music and they both come from ordinary, loving families. Tess's mother and father worked in factories and often struggled to make ends meet. Vernon's father was a lorry driver and his mother worked in department stores.

Vernon and Tess were raised knowing the importance of hard work. When Tess told her parents she wanted to be a model they tried their best to put her off. It was only when she broke into television that they felt confident that she'd made the right decision. For Tess the break came on Channel 4's *The Big Breakfast*. She was later snapped up by children's television and presented shows such as *Smash Hits* and *SMTV Live*. It was during filming on the satellite channel UK Play that she met fellow TV presenter Vernon Kay for the first time.

Vernon was the booming, funny presenter who had made his way into the business from modelling. Before that he'd cleaned phone boxes and been a council caretaker. Vernon and Tess's relationship and careers began to take off. In 2004, Vernon took to the BBC Radio1 airwaves with his own weekend show. He also got to the final in *Ant and Dec's Gameshow Marathon* in a special show of *Family Fortunes*. In 2006, Vernon was named the new presenter of the classic show, now renamed *All Star Family Fortunes*, featuring celebrities and their families.

Meanwhile, Tess has carved out a niche as the glamorous co-presenter of the BBC's hugely popular show *Strictly Come Dancing*. Each week Tess soothes the nervous contestants with her warm and easy-going presence. She is the perfect foil for her co-host Bruce Forsythe. However, at the end of 2006 there

Vernon and Tess are a glamorous TV couple.

were rumours that Vernon Kay may replace Bruce in the future. This suggestion seems more likely after the exciting debut of the husband and wife team on the BBC show *Just the Two of Us*.

"It's rare to have two individuals who are popular and successful in their own right, and as a couple. But these two complement each other. They're popular, good at what they do, great looking and have the whole package. Both seem friendly and genuine on television – that's a rare quality and one the British public loves."

PR man, Max Clifford.
Daily Mirror, November 2006

Other TV Celebrities

Freema Agyeman

When Billie Piper left *Doctor Who* and his Tardis behind, Freema Agyeman stepped into her shoes as Martha Jones, the new assistant to the Doctor. The young actress, who studied Performing Arts and Drama at Middlesex University, has Ghanaian and Iranian parents. Before the part in *Doctor Who*, she played Lola Wise in the soap *Crossroads*. She made her debut as the doctor's new assistant in 2007 in *Smith and Jones*, the first episode of the new series. Keen-eyed viewers recognised her from a previous episode called *Army of Ghosts* in which she played the character Adeola. The producer of the programme was so impressed by her performance that he called her up for a secret audition to be the next assistant. Freema was optimistic about her exciting new role, "Billie rightfully built up an amazing fan base and she will be missed, but I hope the fans are willing to go on new adventures with me."

David Walliams and Matt Lucas

The sketch show *Little Britain* is filled with shocking characters delivering some of the most memorable catchphrases on television. The foul-mouthed teenager Vicky Pollard with her famous "Yes but no but yeah but" catchphrase is played by comic actor Matt Lucas. Carol Beer, the unhelpful bank worker and travel agent who regularly responds with a cough and "Computer says no", is played by fellow comic actor David Walliams. Matt Lucas was born on 5 March 1974 in Middlesex. David Walliams was born on 20 August 1971 in Surrey. They met at the National Youth Theatre and both went on to study drama at the University of Bristol. It was Matt who had the first big break on television. He regularly appeared as the overgrown baby George Dawes on the Vic Reeves and Bob Mortimer comedy quiz show *Shooting Stars*. He has also gone on to appear in straight television dramas such as *Casanova*. David Walliams has appeared in the soap *Eastenders* and the crime drama *Marple*. The duo's first television outing together was in the comedy show *Rock Profile* in 2001 on BBC2. They played spoof versions of rock musicians such as Bono, Kylie Minogue and Ringo Starr. The same year, *Little Britain* was aired on Radio 4. The programme soon caught on and moved to television in 2003. After three series, a Christmas special and a live tour of the show, Matt and David have become some of the most famous faces on television. *Little Britain* has earned them numerous awards and they have been offered a new sketch show for the BBC as well as film deals in the USA. David earned the public's respect in 2006 by swimming the English Channel for the charity Sport Relief, and Matt made a documentary about this.

Jonas Armstrong

Jonas Armstrong, the six-foot Irish actor, is the latest face of the legendary hero *Robin Hood*. In 2006, Jonas burst onto our screens in the BBC's new version of the classic story. Jonas was born on 1 January 1981 in Dublin, Ireland. He was raised in St Annes, Lancashire. At school, Jonas enjoyed doing impressions of his teachers. When he was 17, he decided he wanted to become an actor. He enrolled at London's famous Royal Academy of Dramatic Art (RADA) where he became a classically trained actor. He graduated in 2003 and worked on stage and television. He appeared in the television dramas *Teachers*, *The Ghost Squad* and *Losing Gemma*. *Robin Hood* is his first major role and he didn't expect to get it. Since taking on the part he's had to train in archery, sword fighting and horseriding. Jonas returned as Robin in the second series of *Robin Hood* in 2007.

Dermot O'Leary

Sean Dermot Finton O'Leary was born in Colchester, Essex on 24 June 1973 to Irish parents. After leaving school Dermot attended Middlesex University where he studied for a degree in Media and Television. He began his broadcasting career on BBC Radio Essex, but moved into television in 1999 to present Channel 4's television programme *T4*. His next break came in 2001 when he began presenting *Big Brother's Little Brother*, the spin-off from Channel 4's notorious *Big Brother* programme.

However, there's more to Dermot than a love of music and media. He regularly plays rugby and runs the London Marathon. As a result he was the top option to present BBC's *SAS: Are You Tough Enough?* (2002), *SAS Jungle* (2003) and *Dermot's Sporting Buddies* (2002). Dermot's cheeky wit and easy good looks ensured he attracted the female fans. However, he was also winning music fans on his XFM radio shows. In 2004 he went mainstream and joined the ranks of Radio 2, where he presents the *Dermot O'Leary Show* each Saturday night.

In 2006, Dermot stepped up his game. The BBC chose him to present the new National Lottery show *1 Vs 100*. Then in March 2007, it was announced that Dermot would be the new presenter of ITV's primetime success, *The X Factor*. Apparently, the ex-altar boy from Essex was the number one choice.

Lacey Turner

In the soap *Eastenders*, Lacey Turner plays the feisty and outspoken Stacey Slater. In the famous fictional locale of Albert Square, Stacey has been seen to scheme, lie and even steal. She has also fallen in love and had her young heart broken a few times. In real life. Lacey Turner prefers a quiet night at home watching films with her boyfriend. She still lives with her parents and two sisters in Hertfordshire. Lacey was born on 28 March 1988 in London. At school she attended drama classes each Thursday night. It was in her final year at secondary school that she auditioned for a part in *Eastenders*. Up until then she'd worked in advertisements and theatre. For Lacey, *Eastenders* was the big time! Originally, she was up for a part in the Miller family. but the show's producers wanted her in the show as a Slater. She first turned up in the square in 2004 and soon became the character viewers loved to hate. Lacey's performances have earned her nominations and awards for her acting. In 2006, she won the Best Actress award at the British Soap Awards. The same year *Eastenders* won the Mental Health Media Award for the storyline following the relationship between Stacey and her manic depressive mother.

David Blaine

The American illusionist and stunt performer David Blaine was born on 4 April 1973 in New York, USA. He got his taste for magic when he saw a street performer playing card tricks when he was four years old. Since then, he's gone on to become an international celebrity with his own television shows. David originally became famous as a street magician, performing card tricks and levitation. He had a gift for working the crowds. He sent a tape of his street shows to American television station ABC and was rewarded with a million-dollar contract to produce his own show. *David Blaine: Street Magic* was first shown in 1997, followed by *David Blaine: Magic Man* in 1999.

David has gone on to become one of the most talked about stunt performers of all time. His daring spectacles include being encased in a block of ice for more than six hours, raised on a 90 foot pillar with no food or support for 34 hours, and spending 44 days without food in a transparent plastic cube suspended 30 feet over the River Thames in London. These dramatic stunts were broadcast on news networks around the world and have been the subject of documentaries. David has often been criticised for his life-threatening stunts. More recently, he shocked television viewers by appearing to pull his beating heart from his chest and collapsing on set.

Index

21st Century Lives

Contents of more books in the series:

WAYLAND